THE PHILOSOPHY OF
WINE

THE PHILOSOPHY OF
WINE

RUTH BALL

First published 2019 by
The British Library
96 Euston Road
London NW1 2DB

Text copyright © Ruth Ball 2019
Illustrations copyright © British Library Board 2019
and other named copyright holders

ISBN 978 0 7123 5278 9
eISBN 978 0 7123 6487 4
Cataloguing in Publication Data
A catalogue record for this book is available
from the British Library

Designed and typeset by Sandra Friesen
Printed and bound by Finidr, Czech Republic

CONTENTS

W. r. Senus. fecit. 1808.

Herfst.

INTRODUCTION

THE HISTORY of wine is long and complicated. It spans millennia, continents and all social classes. To know the full story is probably impossible. Yet in your life you will probably meet those people who not only think that they know everything about wine but who will try to make you feel like a failure for knowing less.

To impress them you could try to learn enough of the basics – varietals and DOCs, petits and grands châteaux, conventional techniques and the natural wine movement – to bluff your way along and try to keep up. Unfortunately, if you bluff your way through the first few minutes, that will probably only lead to more discussion along the same lines. Soon you will be lost, bored and eventually discovered.

It's a shame that this is the way it goes. Because, while wine has always had its bores, it also has a history full of life, joy and the various completely ridiculous kinds of things which tend to happen to people who have chosen to dedicate their lives to drink.

This book is about the fun parts of wine history. Once you've read it you can stop that bore in his tracks as he tries to tell you what the best varietals are for the climate in the different parts of Napa Valley by instead asking your companions, 'Did you know that the father of Californian wine was eaten by crocodiles?'

THE GREAT DELUGE

WINE ORIGINATED long before written history, which means that the search for the origins of wine is both difficult and mostly archaeological. In archaeology, luck and serendipity often determine what evidence we find and what is lost forever, leaving us with only our creativity to fill in the gaps. And, no matter what we think we know, there is always the possibility of a new discovery that will turn everything we thought we knew right on its head. But this is the story for now.

For a long time our ideas about ancient foods and drinks were developed from guesswork based on what the shapes of pots and the places where they were found implied to us about their most likely uses. Occasionally, with luck, archaeologists might find more lasting remnants such as bones, fruit pits and grape pips to tell us more about the foods which ancient people ate, but liquids left no traces beyond slight stains, which gave hints about colours. However, in the last thirty years molecular archaeology has allowed us to go beyond guesswork to identify the residues of ancient foods and drinks from little more than just that stain at the bottom of a pottery vessel. These techniques can identify not only the main constituents of a drink, and any additives such as resins or herbs, but also detect the presence or absence of yeast cells. This allows us to identify for certain whether we are dealing with plain grape juice or with the most ancient vintages of wine.

The very earliest evidence for an alcoholic drink containing grapes comes from ancient China, from an excavation site in Henan province. Jiahu was a Neolithic settlement which was occupied from approximately 7000 BC to 5700 BC, a fortified settlement of around forty-five households. The finds from the site are amazingly sophisticated for such an early settlement. They include some inscribed symbols, which may be an early stage in the development of writing, and the oldest known playable musical instruments, flutes which were carved from the hollow leg bones of cranes. But, most intriguingly for the history of wine, a number of pottery vessels were found which had held a fermented alcoholic drink containing grapes, along with rice, honey and a number of different herbs.

It shouldn't be surprising that the earliest discovered fermented drinks were found in China and from a date so much earlier than any evidence of them in the West. The invention of pottery in China preceded any pottery in Europe by as much as 6,000 years, and pottery is the most essential technology for reliable fermentation of any

kind. However, while there were a few grapes in this drink, they aren't the main ingredient – it isn't wine as we know it today. There is also no evidence that the grape was ever domesticated in China. It was rice which developed into the primary source of alcohol for the region. For the origin of wine as a purely grape-based alcohol we have to look further west to the Near East and to Europe.

There are more than seventy species of grapevine growing worldwide but only one came to define wine, *Vitis vinifera*. The species grows wild along the shores of the Mediterranean from the southern tip of Spain. From there the natural range stretched as far north as the Danube river and as far east as the southern shores of the Black and Caspian seas. Throughout that range there is evidence of the wild grape being picked and eaten as food. Wild grape pips have been found mixed with the seeds of other fruits in places where there are signs of habitation which predate the dawn of agriculture, a time when humans were largely nomadic hunter-gatherers. But winemaking requires huge stationary vats for treading the grapes, and also very large numbers of grapes to be gathered together in one place. Even if a suitable trough might have been found, it would have been extremely difficult to get together enough fruit by gathering the widely spread wild grapes. Beyond the odd accidental batch of a few glasses that were the result of attempting to store fruit, true winemaking had to wait for cultivation to produce a stable supply of grapes in a concentrated area.

The domesticated vine and winemaking appear more or less simultaneously in the archaeological record, which suggests that the discovery of wine might have been the primary motivation for the domestication of the grape. The three oldest discovered and identified wine residues in the world are from Godin Tepe, in the middle of the Zagros Mountains and on the western edge of modern Iran, dating back to 3100–2900 BC; from Hajji Firuz Tepe, in the northern Zagros Mountains, dating back to 5400–5000 BC; and from Shulaveri-Gora, a site in the Caucasus Mountains south of the modern capital of Georgia, which has been dated as far back as 6000–5800 BC. The evidence shows that mankind has been making and drinking wine for at least 8,000 years, from almost the very first moment that the pottery and the agricultural knowledge required to make it possible came together.

However, since the few residues which have been identified are so incredibly old, finds from that period are rare. It is always possible, even likely, that the oldest site found so far is only that – the oldest site so far. The chances are that older sites will eventually be found, or that there were older sites but all evidence from them has been washed away by the passing of time. If we assume that the oldest possible site has not been found and may never be found, then more deductive methods have to be used to identify where that first site might have been.

DNA studies have shown that the first domesticated wheat, einkorn wheat, was domesticated and farmed somewhere in the Fertile Crescent, which stretches down the Nile Valley and along the edge of the Mediterranean Sea before following the Tigris and Euphrates rivers down to the Persian Gulf. The single strain of wild wheat which is the closest match to the DNA of modern wheat, and the common ancestor of at least sixty-eight different commonly grown cereal grains, grows in the Karacadağ range of the Taurus Mountains, suggesting that those mountains were where the first wheat grains used for farming came from.

Applying the same technique to the modern vine showed that the oldest domesticated varietals probably arrived in mainland Europe from the Near East but, unlike wheat, no single wild strain was found that matches the modern grapevine. There are plenty of mundane explanations for why this might be: it could be due to the rapid mutation found in grapevines, or the vine may be in an area where samples couldn't be safely collected. One particularly compelling possible explanation was put forward by geo-physicists from Columbia University, William Ryan and Walter Pitman.

In the period 6200–5800 BC, known as the Little Ice Age, there was a significant drop in temperatures worldwide, accompanied by a decline in rainfall. This drove people in the region around the Black Sea to move and settle on its shores so that they could use its water for irrigation. It was perhaps more properly called the Black Lake in that period as, although it was vast, it was also isolated from the sea and so it was filled with fresh water, which was perfect for use by the settlers for their everyday needs. However, when the cold snap ended and the climate warmed again, sea levels rose worldwide and to a level higher than they had reached before the cooling. The barrier between the Black Lake and the Mediterranean Sea was only (at least on a geo-graphic scale) a small land bridge, more like a dam. Once the sea levels rose the dam only had to spring one small leak and it was weakened enough that the whole barrier came crashing down, leaving the Bosphorus channel where the land bridge had been.

Unfortunately, once the lower-lying Black Lake was connected to the ocean, the water level of the lake rose rapidly up to meet sea level and it was forever transformed into the Black Sea. Water flowed through the gap at speeds of up to 80 kilometres per hour, and even in regions on the other side of the lake, miles away from the immediate violence of that rushing torrent, the water would have risen at a speed of 15 centimetres per day, drowning whole villages under a total water level rise of 100 metres.

The geographic evidence for the formation of the Bosphorus is solid, but the idea that the shores of the lake were inhabited when the dam burst has yet to be proven, much less that they were inhabited by the first winemakers. In 2015 a team including Robert Ballard, the underwater explorer famous for discovering the *Titanic*, set out on a grand survey of the floor of the Black Sea to find the drowned villages and to prove that the lake bed was the site of the first vineyards. To date he has discovered over sixty shipwrecks, many of which are of huge archaeological significance, but not a single village.

Nonetheless, the idea that the first wine was made on those shores and that the vines, as well as the knowledge of winemaking, spread out from that point with the refugees as they fled the great deluge has great appeal as a story. It sounds a lot like the story of Noah, who landed in the mountains after a great flood and whose first act on dry land was to plant a good vineyard. He was also found drunk and naked in his tent by his sons, but they tend to skip over that part in Sunday school.

ANCIENT WINE AND THE GODS

WE MAY not know the exact story of the birth and the spread of wine, but we do know that wine reached Egypt before the time of the earliest pharaohs and that it was imported to Egypt from areas around the Black Sea, where viticulture had long been established. The taste for imported wine among the highest ranks of Egyptian society played a key role in the establishment of some of the first successful vineyards outside the native range of the grapevine.

King Scorpion I ruled Upper Egypt around 3150 BC, just prior to the unification of the country under the pharaohs. He was part of what is sometimes called Dynasty 0, the kings from before the first true dynasty of pharaohs. His tomb in the necropolis of the early kings at Abydos was dug down into the ground (he ruled long before the time of the pyramids), and it took the form of a funerary house. The house had many rooms, filled with different offerings representing all the things the king would need to live a comfortable afterlife. One of the rooms was a dedicated chamber filled with nothing but wine, so it must have been important to him to drink well. It was found to contain around 700 jars of wine, stacked several layers deep, to provide the king with enough to drink at every feast in the afterlife.

This would have been an expensive honour, maybe an indicator of expensive tastes in life as well as in death, since an analysis of the pottery found that all of the jars were imported. The clay matched samples from the Gaza Strip, the Hills of Judea and the Jordan Valley, and the wine had almost certainly originated there as well as the clay, since it would have been most efficient to put it into local pots for transportation. Wine had become important enough, or enough of a status symbol, for the king to be buried with it, but despite the demand it was not yet being produced in Egypt. With such enthusiasts at the very highest level of society, however, it would not be long before the Egyptians found a way to transplant the vine to the delta and to start producing wine themselves.

King Scorpion's wine jars were unlabelled and had to be identified from their shape and contents, but in the tombs of the pharaohs of Dynasties 1 and 2 (around 3100–2700 BC) wine jars were found sealed with clay stoppers marked with hieroglyphs, which denote that the wine belonged to, or was made for, the pharaoh himself. These are the first known wine labels in the world and the information included on them is as basic as might be expected. The pharaoh's ownership or control is the main feature, but there are also some hints at the location where the wine was produced that suggest it could have been in Egypt. One label indicates a vineyard which is dedicated to the god Horus and it seems likely that such a vineyard would at least have been Egyptian owned. Another seal points to some kind of relation to the city of Memphis, the capital. However, these hints are sufficiently vague that we cannot say for certain that the wine was made in Egypt.

We know that, by the beginning of Dynasty 4, around 2600 BC, there were certainly vineyards in Egypt and that they were no longer all under the direct control of the pharaoh. Metjen, one of the high officials of the first pharaoh of the dynasty, boasted proudly in his tomb of the walled vineyard on his estate where he produced 'a great deal of wine'. By the time of Dynasty 6, after the builders of the Great Pyramids had come and gone, the set list of offerings for the dead included not just Egyptian wine but wine from five different specified wine regions within the Nile Delta: northern, abesh, sunu, hamu and imet.

Wine importation did not cease with the growth of domestic vineyards, however, and imported wine added variety to the native produce. The drinking cultures of Sumer and Mesopotamia certainly produced plenty of fine vintages for the Egyptians to import. We often struggle to distinguish in their own texts between grape wine, date wine and beer, as the terms for them are often used

interchangeably, but all of them were included in most of the written works from those cultures, from codes of law to the very earliest literature.

The city of Ur was already over 700 years old when the Egyptians began writing wine labels. By the time vineyards were established in Egypt, the city of Ur was at the heart of the Mesopotamian empire and beginning to develop the first literature, which included mentions of wine from the very beginning. Enheduanna, a high priestess of Ur, became the first named poet in history. Her poems, which praised the various temples of the Mesopotamian empire, included lines such as:

Shrine which Enlil loves, place where An and Enlil determine destinies, place where the great gods dine, filled with
great awesomeness and terror: all the Anuna gods attend
your great drinking-bouts.

Drunken gods were a repeating theme through the myths of
the ancient world. The echoes of that legacy are felt keenly
in modern religions from Christianity, which makes wine
into the very blood of God in Communion, to Islam, which
bans drinking outright in this life but promises rivers of
wine in the next. While we would now think it strange to
be drunk in a place of worship, drinking with the gods was
once a fine tradition.

Most Egyptian religious festivals involved some drinking
and most sodden of all was the Festival of Drunkenness,
which was dedicated to the dual goddess of Sekhmet and
Hathor. Beer was the drink of choice at this festival, even for
the rich, as it commemorated a trick played on the goddess
with beer. Sekhmet was a goddess of destruction who had
flown into a rage and determined to destroy all of humanity, but her fellow gods distracted her by colouring 7,000
jars of beer red and pouring in into a field until the whole
field was filled with beer three hands high. She believed
that it was human blood and drank it with joy, only to fall
asleep drunk. When she awoke it was as the peaceful goddess Hathor. To celebrate, the people drank beer all night,
trying to outdrink Sekhmet, until they fell asleep and were

woken at dawn to worship Hathor by priests loudly banging drums.

Wine, on the other hand, was dedicated to the god Osiris, whose story of death and rebirth bears a striking similarity to the story of the later Greek god Dionysius. Although there was a lot of wine drinking at his festival there was one even more drunken occasion connected with wine, although it sometimes didn't take place for thirty years at a time. A large quantity of shards from labelled ostraca (storage jars for various liquids) were found on the site of the palace of Pharaoh Amenhotep III. The wine ostraca listed the regions and years of production of their contents as well as the occasion for the presentation of the wine to the pharaoh. Labels included 'wine for offerings', 'wine for taxes' and 'wine for a happy return', which might have been from someone returning after a long time away. However, the vast majority of the shards were for wine with a single purpose, the heb-sed.

A pharaoh's first heb-sed did not take place until the thirtieth year of his reign, but after that it took place every three years. The main purpose of the festival was for the pharaoh to prove that he remained strong and vital enough to rule over Egypt, even in his old age. In addition to managing to drink and distribute more wine than had been drunk in the palace over the whole of the previous three years put together, the king had to run three times around a set course to prove his fitness to the watching crowds.

Whether he did this drunk or sober is uncertain. Amenhotep III also developed the festival further during his reign. As part of the celebration he sailed a boat, accompanied by statues of the gods, across a vast artificial lake which he had ordered be constructed at his palace.

As the power of Sumer and Egypt waned, and first Greece then Rome rose as the dominant power in the Mediterranean, the idea of wine acting as a link to the gods at their festivals remained strong. The Greek god of wine was Dionysius, who was also the god of women, slaves and outcasts. His mystery cult held ecstatic ceremonies where his priestesses took on the spirit of the god, sending themselves into a trance with wine drinking and rhythmic dancing. His public festival centred around a procession of phalluses, since he was also a fertility god, and of women carrying and distributing wine to the gathered crowds.

On Dionysius' day the normal rules of society fell away as wine returned the participants to their wild, primordial nature. When the Romans ruled Greece they thought this liberation of women and slaves was so dangerous that they suppressed the cult, but it survived on the outskirts of society. Eventually it was absorbed into the Roman canon as the cult of Bacchus, with a new name but the same rebellious spirit as well as the same congregation of women and drunken, ecstatic feasts. The Romans still feared the excesses of the Bacchanalia so much that in 186 BC they officially limited the gatherings to no more than five people, on

1522 D✶V SEPT 14

penalty of death. However it was the liberal element of the festival that they feared rather than the drunken one. At the Saturnalia, the feast of the god for whom Saturday is named, the Romans drank and feasted non-stop for six days.

For the Romans drinking was also an everyday affair, and theirs was the first writing that described wines from certain regions being imported and valued for their specific tastes and characters. Many of the most valued wines were sweet white wines from Greece, which were made by letting the grapes dry on the stalks until they were almost raisins before treading. Falernum was the native star of the wine-growing areas near Rome, and was grown in a select area halfway between Rome and Naples in three different styles: dry, sweet and light. Mamertine was the best wine from Sicily and from the northern reaches of Italy came Rhaeticum, Preatutium and Hadrianum.

The taste for very sweet wines in general seems odd to us today, but the preference was probably to do with which wines kept best without the benefits of modern cellars. The wines would also have been drunk watered down and spiced; to drink unwatered wine was a sign of a savagery and thought to drive drinkers mad. Finally, and also to help the wines keep, almost all Roman wines had tree resin added to them, in common with most wines in the ancient world. In Egypt they had imported terebinth resin especially for the purpose, but the Romans used a range of different resins. The idea of resinating wine now mostly

brings to mind Retsina, which still includes pine resin and is not the most popular of wines around the globe. However, the idea of adding an element from a tree for flavour shouldn't seem so strange, as the practice died out only when we began storing our wines in wooden barrels. Where the Romans had wines which were resinated, we have wines which are oaky, having picked up flavours from the barrels.

DEVELOPING TECHNOLOGIES

THE ROMANS, the Greeks and most of the more ancient cultures before them all used the same vessel for the storage and transportation of wine, the amphora. An amphora is an upright clay jar with a pointed tip and two large handles, which can hold between 20 and 40 litres of wine. It took two men to carry one – in fact the name literally means 'something which can be carried by two' – and special stands were required to keep them upright in homes and taverns. When shipping, they were packed upright into a deep layer of sand which filled the entire floor of the hold.

The wooden barrel for storing wine was invented by the Celts around the first century BC, a while after the Romans had introduced wine-growing to Gaul. Made from northern-growing oak, it was superior to the amphora in almost every way and swiftly replaced it not only for the storage and transportation of wine, but also for almost all bulk goods from oils to gold coins. Barrels were lighter, they were sturdier and their shape allowed one man to roll

a barrel which was too heavy to be lifted. They could also be easily stacked for shipping or storage.

There was one disadvantage to barrels, however. When made from the right kind of clay, the amphora was airtight, allowing wine to be stored and aged for long periods. Wooden casks, on the other hand, are watertight but do allow in small amounts of air. For the ageing of spirits this breathing is an advantage, and it is for wine as well for a short period, but any attempts to store wine for long periods would result in vinegar. Despite this problem, the advantages of the use of casks, not to mention the delicious oaky flavour they imparted, outweighed this one disadvantage and the ageing of wine became a forgotten technique for over a thousand years.

The woodworking skills which created the barrel also allowed the stone troughs in which wines had traditionally been trodden to be replaced with wooden treading vats. The majority of ancient wines were white wines because the stone troughs were often too shallow or too few in number for the grape juice to be allowed to be left to ferment on the skins and stalks, which is how red wine is produced. Instead the grapes would be trodden and then the juice would be rapidly drawn off to ferment in large clay jugs. With the advent of wooden treading vats, it became easier to build more and deeper vats where the wine could ferment on stalks. There was one slight disadvantage – the larger vats sometimes suffocated the treaders if the wine began to

Dubois *del*   J. Marchand *direx.*

Ier CAHIER D'ETUDES

A Paris chez Basset. Rue St Jacques N.º 65.

ferment before the treading was finished and the vat slowly
filled with carbon dioxide – but despite the dangers, red
wine still became widely popular.

Another advantage was the great range of sizes of barrel which could be made, from tiny compact barrels for
travellers to vast storage tuns for the rich to show off their
wealth of wine. These huge tuns would stay in place in the
cellars of richer wine drinkers, being regularly topped up
from deliveries of more sensibly sized barrels, and there
was great competition for the prestige of having the largest
tun. One of the most famous is the Heidelberg Tun, which

was first constructed in the cellars of Heidelberg Castle in Germany in 1591. It has been replaced four times since, and remains a tourist attraction to this day. It has a capacity of over 200,000 litres, although it is no longer kept full of wine, and still has axe marks where soldiers in the Second World War tried to drain it. They were disappointed, as it proved to be empty.

The earliest recorded giant tun was built by the monks at Eberbach Abbey in Burgundy in the year 1500 to celebrate their status as the largest producer in the region. It contained over 70,000 litres and was described as the eighth wonder of the world. It may also have been too much of a temptation, as in 1525 the local people stormed the abbey, plundering it of both its wealth and its wine.

The same woodworking techniques which made the construction of huge barrels possible also allowed the invention of a key piece of technology in the development of wine: the wine press. These huge, mechanical presses allowed for as much as 20 percent more juice to be extracted from grapes than was produced by treading alone. The wine was thought to be of lower quality – the higher level of tannins extracted from the pressing made the wine bitter – but the economic advantages of more wine, even if it was lower-quality wine, were obvious.

Unfortunately, the capital expenditure required to build the huge presses was high and so they were generally found only on large estates owned by the Church or by the

Het Heydelberger Wyn-vat.

nobility. However, tenants might be allowed to use their landlord's press in exchange for a share of the crop. The reputation of press wine would only change from a lower-quality by-product to an essential element of fine wine with the invention of the next key piece of winemaking technology, the bottle.

Blown glass was an old technology, but the glass it made was thin, fragile and expensive. It was sometimes used for small scent bottles or serving bottles for wine which, like the jugs more generally used for service, could be refilled from the cask, but it was a luxury that was unsuitable for the mass storage or transportation of wine. The heavy, dark glass bottle which was suitable for storing both wine and beer was invented in England in the mid-seventeenth century by Sir Kenelm Digby, an author, alchemist and courtier at the court of King Charles I prior to the Civil War and the king's execution.

The manufacture of the thicker, stronger bottle was made possible by a new technique for getting a coal furnace to a much greater heat, successfully melting glass with less potash and lime, the elements which made glass fine but fragile. The darkening of the glass was an unavoidable side-effect of the coal fumes, but it actually had the fortunate property of protecting wine from light. Modern glass production techniques allow for the production of perfectly clear bottles suitable for wine, and they are often used for white or rosé wines; for reds we now add artificial colour back into the glass to replicate that useful accidental property of the earliest wine bottles.

The first glass wine bottles were sealed with a ground glass stopper, which had to be handmade to fit the particular bottle perfectly, as the hand-blown bottles were never quite regular. This made the bottles still very expensive for use with wine. It was the rediscovery of the cork stopper, which the Romans had sometimes used to seal amphoras, which allowed the wine bottle to become the universal symbol of wine which it now is. With the invention of the bottlescrew in the late seventeenth century, or corkscrew as it would later be known, which allowed corks to be pushed fully inside the neck, the bottles could also be racked on their sides to keep the cork damp and fully air-proof.

OCTOBER.

Es quillt, aus diesem Faß, die Geistes-Milch der Greisen,
der Sorgen Gegengift, der Weisheit trinkbars gold.
das Leben würde Tod, die Lust erloschen heißen;
wann der October uns so viel nicht schenken wollt.

At last wine could be safely and routinely aged again, for the first time since the Romans. It was also at this time that the wine press came into almost universal use. The extra tannins it produced, which were so unwanted in new wine, would mellow into perfection in aged wines.

V.—Preparation of Champagne.

NEW WINE, NEW TASTES

WITH THE invention of the bottle the birth of whole new categories of wine became possible, even against the will of their accidental creators. Dom Pierre Pérignon was a Benedictine monk who was appointed treasurer of Hautvillers Abbey in 1668. On his appointment he began a lifelong quest to improve the wines that they produced from their own small vineyard of 25 acres, as well as from the tithe of an eleventh of the harvest which they collected from other vineyards in the area.

Dom Pérignon's first act was to do away with the practice of collecting tithes in trentins, small casks which had to be sent to the abbey packed tightly with treaded grapes. These inevitably produced a rough red wine as a result of the long contact that the treaded juice had with the skins on their journey to the abbey. To ensure that the correct proportion of grapes was sent to the abbey the growers also had to tread the rest of their grapes into similar casks, ruining their own proportion as well. Many would prefer to pay their tithe in money and by accepting that Dom Pérignon gained the funds to buy grapes from only the best vineyards in the area.

White wine, still and with a delicate flavour, was what Dom Pérignon wanted to produce. Unfortunately, the early, cold winters in the northerly Champagne region where the abbey was located had a tendency to stop the fermentation of the grapes early. Then, when the wine should have been ready to drink in the spring, it began fermenting again in the warmth of the changing season, leaving the wine fizzing in the cask. He found this completely unacceptable and worked to reduce this tendency with every method that he had at his disposal.

His golden rules for winemaking, which were prescribed in writing for all winemakers at the abbey by the time of his death, began with the use exclusively of red pinot noir grapes. They were both delicately flavoured and produced a juice with less tendency to secondary fermentation than that of white grapes. Secondly, the grapes were never to be treaded with feet but instead were to be placed intact into a winepress to allow the juice to run free of the skins immediately, taking as little colour from them as possible. Lastly, the wine was to be racked repeatedly to get it off the lees, which might contribute to that secondary fermentation. His methods must have worked, as by 1700 the wines from Hautvillers Abbey commanded double the average price for the region and were regularly shipped to the court in Paris.

It was in London that the fashion for drinking the wines of Champagne in an abominably sparkling state began. In 1661, the Marquis de Saint-Evremond, a minor French noble, ex-soldier, satirist and noted *bon vivant*, fled Paris and exiled himself in London after he was threatened with imprisonment in the Bastille for a satirical public letter he had written about Cardinal Mazarin, King Louis XIV's prime minister. He took with him several casks of still wine from the Champagne region, which was all that he and his fashionable friends would drink. When the wine proved popular with his new, equally fashionable friends in London, he ordered more to be shipped to him and quickly became the unofficial agent for champagne in London.

His new batch of champagne was shipped as soon as possible after the new harvest. It was the fashion in England to bottle all wines on arrival rather than leave them in the cask, as was the practice still in France, and so he had the wine transferred straight into the new, strong English bottles. He probably had no idea what would happen to the wines, sealed up in their bottles without any outlet for the gases from the secondary fermentation that kicked off in the spring. When they were finally opened the wines came out distinctly fizzy. The marquis was appalled, but his new friends were delighted, especially when they discovered an increased uninhibiting effect which came with the bubbles. Modern science has proved what they suspected: the bubbles in champagne cause you to absorb the alcohol more quickly and to get drunk faster.

The fashion for sparkling champagne only truly took off in France with the regency of Philippe, Duc d'Orléans, replacing the still, perfumed wine of Father Pérignon. The duc was a notorious hedonist who had purchased the world's largest diamond from an English merchant in 1717 for £135,000 (the equivalent of over £15 million today). It was purchased from the National Treasury and became part of the crown jewels of France, but it is still known as the Regent Diamond today. At the great banquets he hosted, which he privately referred to as orgies, he drank sparkling champagne in vast amounts. It was largely due to his life of champagne-drenched hedonism that champagne gained

MADAME VEUVE CLICQUOT AT EIGHTY YEARS OF AGE.

(From the Painting by Léon Coignet.)

p. 64.)

THE CLICQUOT-WERLÉ ESTABLISHMENT AT REIMS.

the image of luxury and decadence which it enjoys today. However, the fizz in those early champagnes would have been gentle and the wines a little cloudy too. It took the additional invention of a method to remove the lees from the bottle without losing too much wine or carbonation by Veuve Clicquot, or the widow Clicquot, in 1815 to finally truly produce the perfectly clear, strongly sparkling champagne which we know and love today.

Another modern famous wine was also born of London tastes and got its start from the interplay between Britain and France. This time it came from the hate side of their eternal love–hate affair. It all started when a special treaty was signed with Portugal in 1703, allowing Portuguese wines to be shipped to Britain at a specially reduced rate of tax. Something was required to replace the French wines whose import was banned while the countries were at war. Because of the greatly increased shipping distance – wines were still shipped in cask and bottled only on arrival – the wine often arrived tasting sour and bitter.

None of the wines were thought to be much good, but the best of the bad lot was the full-bodied and heavily tannic wine which English shippers had bought at the port of Oporto at the mouth of the Douro river. Despite the poor quality of the wine, it was still popular with tavern drinkers as it was cheap and, with the addition of some spirits to help it keep through the journey, it was powerful too. Since relations with France showed no sign of improvement, English merchants began setting themselves up in Oporto and journeyed up the Douro in search of better wines, purchased directly from the producers rather than from the Portuguese merchants at the river mouth.

The upper reaches of the valley, where the best wine came from, were difficult to navigate. Violent rapids showed up suddenly between long placid stretches of river. They could be navigated with skill and nerve going downstream, but going upstream the only option was to get out and walk, carrying your boats with you. For Thomas Woodmass, one of the merchants who wrote extensively about his travels in the valley, the journey to Portugal was no picnic either. On the Channel crossing the ship he was travelling on was first captured by French privateers and then recaptured by English ones. Next, as he was travelling down the coast towards Portugal, he was captured again by pirates, of the less state-sanctioned variety, and had to be rescued for a second time, but he did eventually make it up the river to start his hunt for a better wine.

Despite their adventures, the English traders succeeded not only in finding the best vineyards at the upper end of the Douro Valley, but also in persuading the growers there to improve their methods. They imported casks for them to use instead of the traditional skins that wines were previously transported in, since Portugal is well out of the natural range of the oak tree. This was a great improvement in itself. However, it was the discovery in the early nineteenth century that adding brandy before the fermentation was complete halted the fermentation early, leaving a sweeter wine which matured beautifully in the bottle, which truly elevated port from a product of necessity to the fine wine it is today.

With the wines of the Madeira Islands it wasn't necessary to add spirits prior to the end of fermentation to produce a sweet result. Madeira had been small, uninhabited group of islands just off the northern coast of Africa, which were settled by the Portuguese in the mid-thirteenth century. It came to prominence in the mid-seventeenth century when it found itself the last stopping-off point on the trade route to the Americas. It was an obvious place for Portuguese ships headed for their possessions in Brazil to take

WINE BOATS AT OPORTO.

on supplies, but it was also made a key exception to the rule that British colonies in North America could only be supplied by ships from England. Any other wine going to British colonies had to be trans-shipped from Europe via England, with the increased costs that involved, but Madeira wine could be transported directly.

The style of wine produced in Madeira was influenced by the local climate. The grapes were allowed to dry on the vines in the hot sun after ripening until they were nearly raisins, producing a much sweeter wine in a style which the Romans might have recognised. It was also noted that the high acidity of the wines allowed them to actually improve with the first stages of oxidisation, but if the process went too far they would still turn to vinegar like any other wine.

THE VINTAGE AT MR. LEACOCK'S QUINTA AT SÃO JOÃO, NEAR FUNCHAL, MADEIRA.

At first the primary use for the wine was for the sailors to drink on their journey to prevent scurvy, and to provide wine of any kind to the settlers in the new colonies. It kept better than other wines on the journey, but still not well enough to arrive in the Americas in good shape.

It was the opening up of trade routes to India which brought about the transformation of Madeira into a fortified wine. Before the opening of the Suez Canal in the late nineteenth century, ships journeying from Europe to India had to travel all the way down the western coast of Africa, around the Cape of Good Hope, and then all the way back up the other side towards the Indian coast. The only hope for keeping any wine drinkable over the six-month journey, through hot weather and rough seas, was the addition of a good quantity of brandy. With most wines this would give

THE ARMAZENS AND COOPERAGE OF MESSRS. COSSART, GORDON, & CO. AT FUNCHAL, MADEIRA.

them some hope of coming through the journey just about palatable, but with Madeira something odd happened. It seemed that, once fortified, the heat and the other abuses of the journey actually made the wine taste better instead of worse. It arrived in India with a deeper, richer flavour than before and the arrival of the latest shipment was soon eagerly awaited.

It didn't take very long for the fashionable crowd in London to hear about this luscious new wine arriving in India, but direct shipments from Madeira continued to arrive in England without the promised depth of flavour. The revelation that the journey was what gave the wine its unique flavour opened up a new market for ship-aged wines. Huge, extra-strong barrels were made especially to be stored in the bilges of the East Indiamen as they made their journey all the way to India and back again, crossing the equator four times on the way. It seemed that, however much abuse they suffered, including being submerged in the dirty water of the bilges for much of the route, the wines returned all the better for their journey.

However, shipping the wines across continents and back was an expensive business and wine merchants quickly began to look for shortcuts. One London merchant tried ageing the wine in the bottle by burying it in warm horse manure for six months, but that was unlikely to catch on when his customers discovered his methods. Ultimately, the merchants on Madeira decided that heat was the key factor, not the salt water or the rocking of the boat. They built huge ageing lodges called estufas, which were heated to stifling temperatures with great coal-fired stoves.

The new heated wines were, of course, criticised by connoisseurs for not being the same as well-travelled wines. But as the years passed and Madeiras were shipped to London which had been kept in the estufa for ten or fifteen years, much longer than they could realistically hope to spend on a ship, the drinkers of fine wines came around to the idea of artificial heating. The wines produced by the estufas had such great powers of preservation that bottles over a hundred years old have been opened and found to still be sweet, full of flavour and highly enjoyable to drink.

CONVICT-MADE

GENERALLY SPEAKING, everywhere that the British landed where wine could be grown they grew it as one of the very first crops. Perhaps it was the inability to grow wine at home which gave British colonists such an immediate enthusiasm for viticulture. The first governor of the New South Wales colony in Australia was no exception. He brought vines with him when he first arrived with a party of convicts and soldiers to clear the land and to establish the colony. However, for whatever reason, those first vines didn't take and by the time they died the colony was having such problems with the control of alcohol that it didn't seem like such a good idea to start producing home-grown wine.

The very first party of convict-settlers were given a standard rum ration during the journey. The ship had stopped off in Brazil and picked up some particularly rough stuff, probably a cachaça rather than what we would now call a rum. It was a terrible omen of things to come when the double ration issued to everyone to celebrate the successful establishment of the colony resulted in riotous debauchery followed by agonising hangovers for convicts and supervising soldiers alike.

Once the colony was properly established, and there was a supply of clean water, the convicts were no longer allowed rum, while the soldiers who watched them remained well supplied. Maintaining those rules went fine while the initial, well-disciplined, naval men were manning the colony. However they were soon replaced by the New South Wales Corps, who arrived on the second and third fleets along with the first free colonists. Far from being a well-disciplined force, the New South Wales Corps were made up of the dregs of other regiments, including a large group of deserters and one actual mutineer. The men of the corps quickly spotted the opportunity for profit which lay in a monopoly on drink and soon earned themselves the nickname of the Rum Regiment.

Supplies were arriving at the colony not just with the convict ships but also with independent traders. They had heard that the new residents were willing to pay prices high enough to render even the long journey made on spec more than worthwhile. The officers in the colony were permitted to buy goods from the visitors only for their own use, but those regulations were blatantly ignored and soon the colony was awash with spirits, settlers and convicts alike. The governor tried to solve the problem by opening the first legal pubs under strict licence, but the drinking only increased. The governor was replaced and the colony left under the control of the Rum Regiment's major for three years, while the governor returned to Britain and his replacement made the journey back.

By the time the new governor arrived spirits had become the main currency of the colony. He was none too pleased with the situation he discovered. The regiment had established an effective monopoly over not just the spirit supply but also the labour of the convicts, all for their own gain. Unfortunately, he had little opportunity to make changes as a sophisticated whisper campaign, by postal correspondence with London, caused the new governor to retire in disgrace after just five years. It was an impressively short span considering that a return correspondence with London took a year. The man who had orchestrated the campaign was Captain John Macarthur, who had fought three duels with the governors of New South Wales to date, and on his arrival the next new governor, Philip King, immediately had Macarthur sent back to London to be court-martialled.

Macarthur's London connections were still working as well for him now as they had during his whisper campaign. He was not only found innocent at his court martial, helped by the fact that most of the evidence against him had been mysteriously stolen on the voyage, but also returned to Australia with a land grant of 5,000 acres and some of the king's own merino sheep. He had returned to Britain with tales of the suitability of Australia for raising sheep and promised that he could breed enough to save it from the wool shortages the country was experiencing due to the war with France. It was a promise worth taking the risk on. However, the authorities weren't entirely blind to the colony's struggles and they also sent another new governor, Captain William Bligh, to take over command. Bligh was a man famous for a wide range of accomplishments, but was also infamous for having been the commanding officer who had provoked the mutiny on the *Bounty*.

Bligh and Macarthur were at war from almost the first moment that they set foot on shore. Macarthur attempted to further solidify the monopoly of the Rum Regiment by bringing in a pair of copper stills, an item which had been specifically prohibited from import by Bligh. To demonstrate that his control of the colony was greater than the governor's, Macarthur dragged the customs officer, appointed by Bligh, who had seized the stills before a court, claiming that the seizure was unfair. The case was blatantly against him, and the ban on stills was both legal and clear, but the judge advocate, Richard Atkins, was well in Macarthur's pocket due to being a habitual drunk who Macarthur kept well soaked. He was often inebriated in court and had even been known to pass death sentences while too drunk to stand. The court found in the captain's favour, ruling that the stills should be returned to their owner immediately.

Bligh may have lost the fight over the stills but he retaliated by having Macarthur arrested and charged with sedition when one of his ships was found to have a runaway convict on board. The arrest of their ring-leader was the last straw for the Rum Regiment and they staged a coup, arresting and imprisoning the governor at dinner. It was the only military action the corps ever engaged in and Bligh was kept under house arrest while the Rum Regiment ruled Sydney chaotically. Their rule lasted for a number of years before two warships and a regular army regiment arrived to put an end to the rebellion and replace the New South Wales Corps entirely, sending the Rum Regiment home. A warrant for the arrest of John Macarthur was issued in Sydney, but he fled to London to escape arrest, following his son who he had sent to strengthen his case with his business associates but who tragically died not long after his arrival.

Macarthur's refusal to face arrest or any punishment for what he had done, placed him in a self-imposed exile, which he spent touring Europe and looking at vineyards. He eventually gained the right to return provided that he admit his wrongdoing and make a promise of good behaviour. He refused to do even that and waited until he was granted an unconditional pardon in 1817 before finally returning to Australia.

Despite his refusal to promise good behaviour Macarthur returned with vine cuttings and went about setting up Australia's first commercial vineyard peacefully. Most of the early wines produced were a reflection of the early influence of the Rum Regiment and the demand and drinking culture

which they had created. What was produced was mostly fortified wines, with brandy from the stills that Bligh had tried to ban, and the stronger the better. It took over a century for Australia to overcome its reputation for producing nothing but harsh, strong wines despite the fact that there were always some beautiful wines being produced alongside the strong commercial styles.

Today Australia's wines are amazing in their wide range of styles and grape varieties. The great diversity of grapes and vines available in the country, despite the long distance from their countries of origin, is almost entirely due to one man: James Busby.

* * *

Busby arrived in 1824 at the age of 23, with a great passion for winemaking, having written a full book on the subject on the voyage from London. He served his required service as a school teacher at an orphanage and then started his own farm, but he didn't plant the vineyard he had dreamed of immediately because he wasn't satisfied with any of the vines which were available in the country. Returning to Europe, he toured the continent and eventually returned with no fewer than 570 grape varieties which survived the journey. He gave a specimen of each to the Sydney Botanic Gardens and planted the rest to form his own vineyard and nursery. The area where he chose to plant his vineyard turned out to be one of Australia's best wine regions, the Hunter Valley, and he spent his life working to improve the quality of local viticulture and of all the vines on the continent.

It remains a peculiarity of the country that almost all of the early wine pioneers in Australia were enthusiastic Englishmen who had to learn viticulture from scratch rather than colonists from wine-producing countries. This has perhaps led to the great willingness to innovate and to challenge traditional methods of winemaking, which is still a prominent feature of Australian wine culture.

GOLD RUSH, WINE RUSH

When European colonists first arrived in the Americas they were astonished to find vines growing wild every-where. Such abundance, they thought, was bound to make this a new land overflowing with wine. In honour of that prospective future an island off the coast of Quebec, now the Île d'Orléans (Island of Orléans), was originally named Bacchus Island. But the dream of a Bacchic paradise was short-lived. They soon discovered that the grape which grew in the northern parts of the continent where the English had settled, *Vitis labrusca*, was good for eating and for making jellies and juice, but made almost undrinkable wine.

The governor of the Virginia Company in the early seventeenth century described what his colonists had produced as 'more of an embarrassment than a credit to us' and gave up making wine altogether in favour of relying on imports. Further down the coast towards Florida, in the areas colonised by the French and Spanish, a different species grew, *Vitis rotundifolia*. It made a wine which was somewhat more palatable but still a long way from the refined wines from the ancient vineyards of Europe. In a tactful piece of diplomacy a visiting English trader to Fort Caroline, now Jacksonville, in 1565 described the wine made there as 'refreshing' while also saying that it was the first wine he had drunk in seven months, since there had been none available on the long sea voyage. Perhaps he was trying to save both his relationship with his trading partners and the reputation of his palate by adding that proviso.

Reliance on imported wine in the British colonies was fine at first, although the British government did prevent the colonists importing most goods, including wine, from any-where but Britain, which greatly raised the price. However, once independence had been fought for and won, good relations with France became essential to keep the wine flowing in at a better price. Luckily they had Thomas Jefferson as their ambassador to France who, in the four years he spent there in negotiations from 1785 to 1789, developed a fascination with French wine and with the viticulture that produced it.

While his colleagues back home debated the new constitution and held the first election for president, Jefferson was happily touring the wine regions. He sampled the best vintages and took extensive notes about the situation of the vineyards, the way the vines were tended and more commercial matters like yield and the price of wine produced. To improve American wine production he also sent back extensive samples and cuttings but, without an equally

MR. LONGWORTH'S WINE-CELLARS—CORKING THE BOTTLES.

enthusiastic partner back home, he did not succeed in getting them planted. Eventually he returned to the new United States of America and to less important matters than wine, like becoming the third president.

Despite Jefferson's failures there were some small successes with carefully selected native grapes in the early nineteenth century. The richest man in Cincinnati, Nicholas Longworth, became obsessed with producing an American champagne from American grapes while the nation was gripped with a craze for the drink. The demand, which far outstripped supply, was being met by counterfeits which were supposedly made of turnip juice, honey and brandy. They seemingly came out surprisingly well, as the counterfeit champagne was described by a visiting Charles Dickens as 'a pleasant and harmless drink, a very good imitation'.

Nonetheless, this was not good enough for Longworth, who was convinced that he would find a native grape which would produce good wine. Eventually he settled on the Catawba variety. The wine it produced still had the nasty aftertaste associated with the native grape varieties, which is always described as 'foxy', but it was less strong than in other varieties. He had the idea of trying to ferment the grapes without the skins, which he thought were the source of the taste. It did indeed improve the taste and, with the help of some imported French winemakers, he succeeded in producing a clear, fizzy wine which tasted not at all like champagne. Instead it was reported to taste more like artificial strawberries. By 1850 it was a commercial success both in America and abroad as an exciting new novelty, but it has never entered the ranks of fine wine.

Meanwhile, in California, which was initially under Spanish control and then briefly became part of Mexico before it finally joined the United States in 1848, a Bordeaux native called Jean-Louis Vignes was experimenting with imported grapevines systematically and on a grand scale. Unlike some other early experimenters he didn't use cuttings, which struggled to take in the new soil, but had whole vines shipped across with their roots intact. The vines were packed in moss and potato slices to keep their roots from drying out on the long sea crossing. He planted Cabernet Franc and Sauvignon Blanc, which both thrived in the Californian climate.

His vineyard, Rancho el Aliso, was producing 100,000 gallons of wine a year by 1851 and, unlike the novelty

EVERY TRIUMPH

Catawba wine, it was recognised as real, quality wine. His vines have long since disappeared under the concrete of central Los Angeles, but once the imported vines were shown to thrive in California, other immigrant vintners quickly established themselves across southern California, some bringing their own native varieties with them.

The vineyards continued to expand in response to thirsty demand as thousands rushed to the state in 1848 and in the following year, looking for adventure and to make their fortunes in the great Gold Rush. Later some of those who successfully made their fortunes, as opposed to the thousands who failed, stayed to set up vineyards in their retirement. Among those who aimed for a peaceful retirement among the vines was John Sutter, who had been the owner of the ranch where the very first gold was found in the mill race: the discovery that first sparked the rush.

It was the Gold Rush which really pushed the vines of California up into the less settled northern regions of the state, where the best land for wine production would ultimately be found. The wine which was being made there at the end of the Gold Rush had been planted for volume and was crudely made to slake the highly profitable thirsts of the miners. In the poorly supplied and overcrowded towns of the Gold Rush there were reports of people paying as much as the modern equivalent of $90 for a single egg when supplies ran low, so it was easy to get a good price for wine of any quality.

It was the wine made in the vineyard of the retired General Mariano Guadalupe Vallejo in Sonoma County, just outside the central Gold Rush city of San Francisco, which would catch the attention of the man who would later be called the father of fine Californian wine. That man was Agoston Haraszthy, a noble who had served in the imperial bodyguard of the Austro-Hungarian court until court intrigue forced him to flee the country and go in search of new adventures in the New World.

On his arrival in the United States he started several businesses, including the first steamboat line on the Upper Mississippi, and founded a town named after himself in

Wisconsin. Later he moved to San Diego with his family, where he founded more businesses and served as sheriff for San Diego County. He must have found the life of a lawman not to his liking because he stayed only three years before moving on to San Francisco. There, in partnership with a group of Hungarian metallurgists, he ran a branch of the US Mint. It was going very well until the day that he accidentally vaporised $151,000 of gold by running the smelters too hot. After his trial for embezzlement, at which he was ultimately proved to be an incompetent rather than a thief, he left San Diego and at last made his fateful visit to General Vallejo's vineyard. After tasting the wine produced there he immediately bought a neighbouring vineyard, declaring the wine to have 'potential'.

He proved much better at running a vineyard than running a mint, at least to begin with. He imported vines from Europe, planted them on dry slopes without irrigation and fermented his wines in redwood vats. He produced wines so good that the Californian legislature employed him, in 1857, to write a practical manual for wine production for new planters which was rather boringly called *Report on Grapes and Wines of California*. His sound advice, combined with some juicy financial incentives from the legislature, encouraged many new winemakers to set up in California.

Following the success of his initial report, Haraszthy persuaded the legislature to send him on a tour of Europe to investigate grape varieties and winemaking techniques. His trip produced a second report, *Grape Culture, Wines, and Winemaking*, as well as over a hundred thousand carefully shipped cuttings from 300 varieties of vine. The report was well received and has been credited with laying the foundations for scientific winemaking in America. However, the cuttings had been sent without the agreement of the legislature and they ultimately refused to pay for them when Haraszthy tried to persuade them to purchase the cuttings from him. If this financial setback was not enough, it was about to get worse.

European vines planted in the Americas had often failed to thrive, but this was always assumed to be the result of planting in unsuitable soil or unsuitable climates and the good soil of California proved to be fine and nourishing for *Vinis vinifera*. However, by the mid-1860s Haraszthy's vines were beginning to grow brown and weak, victims of a terrible affliction. The vines were being destroyed by the

phylloxera aphid, the same bug which would ultimately destroy most of the vineyards of Europe.

Haraszthy was unlucky, as phylloxera remained rare in California until after the solution was discovered in Europe during the Great French Wine Blight. With the assistance of a Texan it was discovered that grafting *Vinis vinifera* on to the rootstock of a native Texan grape, *Vinis riparia*, which was completely naturally resistant to the aphids, and later also *Vinis rupestris*, passed on that resistance without changing the flavour of the grapes produced. The technique ultimately saved both the Old World vineyards and the Californian industry, but it was discovered too late for Haraszthy.

He left California for another fresh start in Nicaragua, where he went into partnership to develop a sugar plantation. He never got the chance to complete it as he

CALIFORNIA VINTAGE

CABINET SUTER
J. GUNDLACH
SAN FRANCISCO
CALIFORNIA

RHINEFARM

SONOMA

J. GUNDLACH & CO.

SAN FRANCISCO, CALIFORNIA.

disappeared three years later while travelling by mule to a business meeting. It was thought that he had fallen into the alligator-infested river when attempting to cross it. His body was never found and he was presumed to be dead.

Despite the failure of Haraszthy's own vineyard the techniques he wrote about were sound, with just the addition of grafted roots, and the quality of the soil in the state had been proven. By the time the United States fell under Prohibition in 1919 there were 300,000 acres of vines in California. It might be expected that this would decrease under Prohibition, and certainly the official number of wineries was reduced by more than eighty percent. The only survivors were the small number of wineries which were permitted to continue operating for the production of sacramental and medicinal wines. A sudden market for 'nonintoxicating fruit juice', as explicitly permitted under the Volstead Act, kept the vineyards in business despite the closure of their wineries. The high demand for juice, which could be turned into wine by consumers at home with little danger of arrest, resulted in a constant shortage of the refrigerated train cars that were required to ship the unfermented juice. The need to pretend that the juice would remain juice once it entered consumers' homes was a logistical nightmare for the vineyards, but the acreage of vines managed to actually increase to 400,000 acres by 1923.

A brainwave by the Californian Vineyardists Association in 1926 allowed them to put their dormant winemaking

A Brick of Wine

equipment to use. They had the legality of the proposed new product cleared by the attorney general and soon Vine-Glo wine concentrate hit the shelves across the country. Despite having been officially cleared as legal, the marketing of the product was not at all subtle, with large-type headlines such as 'Legal in your own home'. The 'true-to-type' varieties were also listed as Port, Virginia Dare, Muscatel, Angelica, Tokay, Sauterne, Riesling, Claret and Burgundy, which are certainly not the names of grape juices. The attorney general who had cleared the product left government service and took a job with Vine-Glo in 1929, just after the release of the next great innovation, the solid concentrate Bacchus wine bricks. The marketing slogan called the bricks 'solidified merriment' and they carried labels stating 'In one gallon of plain water produces the most delicious unfermented non-alcoholic grape juice'.

However, the grape juice and the wine produced from grape bricks were probably far from most delicious. By the end of Prohibition Californian vineyards had expanded again to 650,000 acres, but the survival and expansion of the vineyards had come at the cost of loss of quality. Producing grapes to be made into bricks did not inspire growers to go to the care and expense of cultivating the finest vines. The glut of cheap, poor-quality wine gave the state a bad reputation which was hard to dispel. Even though the 1960s and 1970s saw a great revival of fine Californian wine, and though by 1976 California was once again producing such good Chardonnays that they beat French challengers at a blind tasting held at a world fair, the world's general impression of wine from the state was more aptly summed up by a clearly intoxicated Orson Welles slurring his way through an advert for cheap Paul Masson 'Californian Champagne'.

Today, however, it would be rare to find a wine list that does not list a Californian wine on it somewhere. Cheap wines are still produced in bulk in California for sale in supermarkets and on tap in Wetherspoons, but they are at least now refreshing and drinkable rather than Prohibition-era hooch. Meanwhile the quality of the best wines produced in California is excellent and continues to be a constant challenge to Europe never to let its guard down and its standards slip.

THE GREAT WINE BLIGHT

THERE WAS another reason why the vine flourished in California when it had always failed to the east of the Rockies, as the world would soon discover. The soil on the east coast wasn't poor; instead it was harbouring an invader which would devastate and change the vines of the Old World forever.

The first vine pest to cross the Atlantic was a powdery mildew, oidium. It was thought to be related to the potato blight which had already ravaged Ireland, killing thousands. The loss of the grapes was a lot less deadly than the potato famine, but it was still devastating to the smallholding peasant farmers who relied on wine as a cash crop. The disease also spread with incredible rapidity. Only three years after the first appearance of the rot in 1851 the disease had spread to every vineyard in France, as well as infecting much of Italy. The rot even made it as far as the Douro Valley in Portugal. Wine production in France dropped by two-thirds compared to the period before the disease emerged.

The French Society for the Encouragement of National Industry offered a grand reward of 20,000 francs to whoever could discover a cure for the disease. Luckily, a remedy had already been discovered in the 1830s for a similar mildew on peaches. It could be cured on fruit trees by the direct application of a solution of sulphur to the branches before budding, but how could this laborious process be applied to acres of grapevines? A water spray was trialled, but ultimately the best results came from a direct application of solid sulphur as a fine dust. It took two men one day to dust a single acre using bellows and many sacks of the burning dust. The cure had to be applied three times a year, and the distribution of so much sulphur would have been impossible without the newly built railways. However, the hard work paid off as by 1858 the majority of the surviving vineyards were free from the fungus.

The peace was not to last. Just four years later, in the village of Roquemaure on the banks of the Rhône in France, a small patch of vines mysteriously sickened and died. They belonged to M. Borty, who had recently received and planted some native American vines from a friend in New York. His house in the tiny village has acquired the same tragic notoriety as the bakery in Pudding Lane where Thomas Farriner unwittingly started the Great Fire of London by burning down his own house.

The spread of the mystery disease was slow. The following summer, vines in the nearby village of Pujaut began to turn yellow and drop their leaves, but over winter the disease seemed to go into retreat. In 1865 it reawakened and began slowly but surely spreading north. Dead vines which were dug up showed roots which had blackened and crumbled, but with no sign of the cause apart from some occasional yellow spots. The spots were thought to be fungal, like oidium, but they could just as easily have been a consequence as the cause of the decay.

By 1868 local dignitaries in the Hérault, the worst affected region, formed the Commission for Combatting the New Vine Disease with the help of the eminent botanist Jules-Émile Planchon. They went out into the fields in their tailcoats and top hats, with their notebooks and magnifying glasses, to investigate the cause of the disease. The dead vines were uprooted and studied in great detail, but their black, crumbling roots revealed nothing of note. It was only the accidental uprooting of an apparently healthy vine on the edge of the spreading patch of dying vines which revealed the source of the problem. Despite the green appearance of the vine, yellow spots had already developed on the roots and the magnifying glasses of the commission revealed that they were made up of microscopic insects which were latched onto the roots, sucking at the sap of the plant. No insects had been found on the dead vines because they had been abandoned by the hungry invaders, which were already searching for healthy vines to make their next meal.

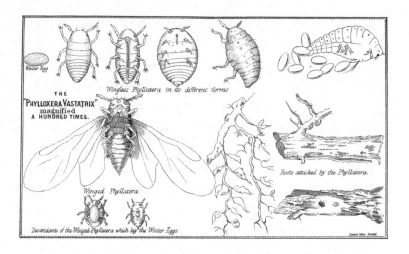

Winter Egg

THE "PHYLLOXERA VASTATRIX" magnified A HUNDRED TIMES.

Wingless Phylloxera in its different forms

Winged Phylloxera

Descendants of the Winged Phylloxera which lay the Winter Eggs.

Roots attacked by the Phylloxera.

Planchon and a colleague at the university identified the form of the insect as similar to the aphid and named it *Rhizaphis vastatrix* (root aphid devastator), but when he sent his field notes to a Parisian expert on the aphid, Professor Victor Signoret, he noted a similarity to an aphid which attacked the leaves of oaks and renamed the insect *Phylloxera vastatrix* (dry leaf devastator). The name stuck, despite the bugs primarily attacking the roots instead of the leaves of plants, and the enemy became generally known as phylloxera.

While scientists debated naming the culprit, the spread of the vine plague continued unabated, both from its original source and from a new, independent infection site on the other side of the country. In 1868 the first patch of vines died in Bordeaux and the following summer 25 acres in the region were affected. Within a year the source of the plague was identified as a harmless minor malady which commonly affected American native vines, but which was deadly to the European variety. The vines of M. Borty were identified as the original source of the infection in the south of France and in Bordeaux the bugs were traced back to the American vines grown proudly and in great variety for twenty years by a M. Léo Laliman.

By 1870 the central government had finally taken notice of the problem, even though Victor Signoret continued to insist that the insect was only a symptom and not the cause of the problem. A commission on the phylloxera was set up and it offered another public prize of 20,000 francs to the person who could cure the disease. It had worked for oidium, so surely science would find a similarly effective cure for the new problem. In the meantime it advised that the spread of the plague should be slowed down or prevented by uprooting and burning any affected vines. Only the mayor of Hérault took this pronouncement seriously, by making it compulsory to uproot and burn any affected vines in his region. He also banned the import of foreign vines to prevent any further outbreaks, but was largely ignored by his citizens.

Meanwhile, further north, war with Prussia came and went and was swiftly followed by revolution and a change of government. The commission continued to sit through the change of administration, the bugs continued to advance through southern France and the prize for a cure remained unawarded. Ideas were submitted, and plenty of them, but they were by and large the untested theories of cranks and amateurs. They suggested that roots be drenched in white wine, tobacco or herb tea. They suggested that fields be planted with strong-smelling plants, with American vines (which they thought the aphids would prefer) or even with toads, buried alive between the rows. The submitted cures were as ineffective as they were unusual, but that didn't prevent many enterprising merchants from making money from their miracle cures by selling them to desperate farmers.

The farmers were growing increasingly desperate, since by 1872 the Hérault was almost completely denuded of vines. Some of the inhabitants even began turning to the very enemy which had inflicted the plague upon them. A number of American varieties of grape were known to be resistant to phylloxera and these were imported by the hundreds to replace the dying vines, bringing even more bugs with them. Meanwhile, a treatment was found which was effective, at least, in halting the advance of the disease. The stay of execution for the treated vineyards came at great financial cost and at serious risk to the vines.

Carbon bisulphide is a thick, noxious liquid which was used at the time in industry to vulcanise rubber. The fumes which it gave off were toxic to humans but also deadly to insects. It had already been found to be of use in killing weevils in grain stores and its promoters were sure that it would also work on phylloxera. The first trial killed the bugs but also resulted in the death of half the vines from poisoning. Tests continued undiscouraged and M. Monestier reported the first successful field trial in 1873 with a lower dose. His victory was only slightly lessened when the bugs returned the following season. In his next attempt he was both poisoned and blown up since the gas was explosive as well as toxic. However, the invention of a giant syringe which could inject the correct dose deep into the soil where the lack of air prevented it from exploding eventually provided a usable, although expensive and risky, treatment. It eventually became popular with the owners of the oldest and best vineyards, who could afford the expensive application three times a year and whose vineyards produced a high-value crop that was worth the expense. They could also to pay someone else to do the dangerous work.

Despite its commercial success, the bisulphide cure did not impress the phylloxera committee because it only suppressed the insect and did not kill it completely. The committee had begun field trials and tested even the strangest of the cures which were sent to them in the desperate hope that something would be successful. Different vines in the trial field were treated with urine (both horse and human), smoke, whale oil, petrol, hot wax and any number of proprietary mystery powders which had been sent to the committee. All of the treatments failed and the prize was increased from 20,000 to 300,000 francs in the hope of inspiring more, and hopefully better, submissions from around the world. More proposals certainly were received, including one to drum the aphids out of the fields with marching bands, but the quality of the submissions did not noticeably improve. The prize remained unawarded.

Léo Laliman, perhaps on a quest for redemption after bringing over some of the insects which were ravaging the ancient vineyards, was convinced that the solution lay with the American vines. He sent a case of wines made from his own crop to the famous scientist Louis Pasteur, who had discovered the existence of the yeasts which cause fermentation, with the hope of recruiting him to his cause. Unfortunately, Pasteur shared the wines with a wine expert of his acquaintance, and they both unanimously pronounced the samples to be inferior to the native wines of France, stating that the very best among them was only as good as *vin ordinaire*, the lowest class of French wine available. A public tasting in Montpellier of both French-produced and imported wines made from American grapes produced the same results. Directly replacing the historical vines of France, in all their famous regional diversity, with these unpalatable American varietals was just not a workable solution.

However, there was one presentation at the same meeting in Montpellier which showed some promise. It was a technique which was already in use in the inhospitable soils of the east coast, where a true French *Vitis vinifera* had been grafted onto the roots of an American vine. It was an experiment in its early stages in France; no wine was available to sample and it would take three years for the new vines to mature and to produce fruit, but the claim that the graft had no effect on the flavour of the grapes was extremely exciting to many delegates, who had just tasted their way through the original products of the American vines.

In the areas which had already been fully devastated by phylloxera there was little to lose by trying the new vines and they took to the grafting technique enthusiastically, developing schools and slowly educating people in the skills required. However, there was a backlash from the areas which were still on the frontier of the fight, which were battling off the bugs with sulphur injections, and from the areas which were still uninfected and hoped to remain so. How could others dream of bringing in more of the deadly American vines which had already wreaked untold devastation on their livelihoods? Two camps emerged: those who wanted to prevent the advance of the plague by controlled burning and with sulphur injections (the *sulferistes*); and those who wanted to reconstruct their vineyards with American vines or grafted vines (the *Américanistes*).

While scientists and administrators divided themselves into opposing camps of opinions the fight on the ground was taking place in vineyards tended by peasants who were both superstitious and suspicious of authority. When the

disease hit Italy local people even blamed the laying of the
great iron tracks of the railways for corrupting the soil and
tore up several miles of track. So when the *sulferistes* won
a great victory with legislation which made the reporting
and treatment, by sulphur application or by burning, of new

infection sites compulsory, it was an extremely dangerous move for a country with more than one revolution within living memory. Enforcers attempting to enter the vineyards to investigate infections were met with pitchforks and strict enforcement was prevented by fears of provoking another popular rebellion.

Still the aphid marched on and, as Burgundy and Cognac found themselves under siege, popular opinion among landowners began to turn towards the *Américanistes*. A chaotic four-day conference held in a rented circus tent in a field in Lyon in 1880 proved a major turning point. The proprietors who had been using sulphur were ready to admit that they were beginning to grow tired of the endless expense and the *Américanistes* were putting forth good arguments from a growing bloc of passionate speakers. The greatest embarrassment for the *sulferistes* came when the final speech of the conference, an interminable rant by M. Pezon of the Lot-et-Garonne Vigilance Committee, was interrupted by the release of a troop of monkeys by the circus owner, who wanted his tent back so he could begin the evening performance. M. Pezon simply continued his rant, apparently unaffected by the spectacle as monkeys whooped and frolicked around him, but he must have looked quite ridiculous.

At a more formal conference in 1881 the arguments went on for so long that the event ran for two full days longer than planned. However, the most anticipated event was the report from a tasting committee who were presented with the first wines produced from French vines grafted onto American roots. They unanimously pronounced the wines to be indistinguishable from the ungrafted varieties. When delegates voted on the last day of the conference, there was a huge majority in support of the removal of the ban on American vines, even though many *Américanistes* had been forced to return home by the overrunning schedule.

By this time France had officially been split into regions. First, in regions which had already been phylloxerated and where the American vines could be freely imported, reconstruction with grafted vines was already taking place. Secondly, in areas which were still free of the bug or still in the first stages of attack, imports remained banned and even the movement of French vines was severely restricted. The *sulferistes* still controlled the central administration and they kept this system in place using subsidies which were given only to sulphur treatment. However, the regions that were declared phylloxerated increased in number year after year, and by 1887, the year that the Côte-d'Or was declared phylloxerated, the *sulferistes* finally gave up the fight. The ban on the import of vines was officially lifted for the entire country and a four-year land tax exemption was declared for newly planted vineyards to support the reconstruction. The exemption covered the time that it would take for the new vines to become productive and for the first vintage to be made.

Reconstruction was a slow and painstaking effort, especially when it came to finding or breeding the right roots for the myriad different soils and conditions in France, as well as in the many other countries phylloxera had spread to, following the original path of the spread of the vine. The plague had spread as far afield as Australia and wherever it went the grafting method soon had to follow. By 1902 the reconstruction in France had been so successful that an excess of wine was actually produced.

The bug itself has, to this day, only been resisted and not defeated. The 300,000 franc prize still sits in gold in the vaults of the Banque de France. Throughout the world you can see the telltale bulge of the graft at the foot of every vine in every field and know that the enemy of the vine is still lurking underground.

SAGE GAIETÉ FRANÇAISE
CHAMPAGNE

WINE AND THE RESISTANCE

WINE IS an essential part of French culture. A survey showed that the appreciation of good wine was considered the fourth most important quality in making people feel French. Only language, birthplace and the defence of liberty were thought to be more important.

When the country fell under occupation during the Second World War the vineyards and cellars of the country, not to mention the expertise of the winemakers themselves, came under threat. Yet, under the threat of imprisonment or even death, the people of the winemaking districts went to great lengths of resourcefulness and ingenuity to try to preserve their culture until a time when their country could be freed and wine restored to its proper place on the table of every true citizen.

The work to protect the great historic vintages for the nation began immediately on the day that war was first declared. The great houses of the Champagne region had barely recovered from the First World War. The war had seen active fighting in the vineyards themselves, an almost

THE CELLIER AND CELLARS OF PÉRINET ET FILS AT REIMS.

sacrilegious act which had left many of them either danger-ously full of unexploded munitions or with soil poisoned by chemical weapons leaching into the ground. The Cham-penoise also remembered the looting they had suffered in the last war and not just from the enemy. French troops had made a habit of helping themselves to cases of champagne as they were on their way to the front to fight and not just in the last war. Many of the limestone caverns which hon-eycomb the land beneath the vineyards still bear Prussian graffiti from the looting which followed Napoleon's defeat at Waterloo over two hundred years ago.

However, the huge, labyrinthine caverns also contained many rooms which were never discovered by looters and even more good hiding places could be produced if a few new walls were built in the right places. The vintners used them to hide not only the best and oldest vintages of cham-pagne before the war began but also guns, furniture and even cars. Marie-Louise de Nonancourt was a widow who had just spent her life savings to buy the run-down vineyard of Laurent-Perrier. With the vineyard had come 100,000 bottles of older vintages, and they were all she had to start up the business, so she was determined to give them some extra protection. She not only built a new wall in her cellar to hide the wine, but she also had a nook built into the wall where she cemented a statue of the Virgin Mary to watch over her investment.

As Marie's vineyard was so run-down, it didn't look too suspicious to have an empty cellar, but in those vineyards that were known to be thriving businesses only the very best wines could be hidden while the rest had to be sacrificed to complete the illusion that there was nothing missing so that looters wouldn't go looking too hard for hiding places. In Burgundy, Maurice Drouhin also had another strategy to make the brand new wall in his cellar look less suspicious. As he built the wall to protect the best of his wines, which included a complete stock of Romanée-Conti from 1929 to 1938, his wife and children ran around the cellar collecting spiders to put in front of the wall where they would spin webs to make the wall look older than it was.

Other parts of the country were more confident that the war would never reach them and so didn't start to build their defences until the Germans breached the Maginot Line in May 1940. Claude Terrail, the son of the owner of the famous Parisian restaurant La Tour d'Argent, flew home with only six hours of leave from the air force in Lyon to try to save his father's legacy. His father had already left Paris, unable to face the horrors of war again after his time as a prisoner of war in the last conflict. But Claude wasn't going to give up, and planned to save as much as he could of his father's pride and joy. The world-famous cellar contained over 100,000 bottles, including many from the previous century. He chose 20,000 of the most precious bottles, one in five and, with the help of the staff, he rapidly walled them in. When he returned to the air force the restaurant was left in the capable hands of the manager and long-time friend of the family, Gaston Masson.

When German forces marched into Paris a month later on 14 June, La Tour d'Argent was the first stop for none other than Hermann Göring himself. He immediately asked to see the cellars, and the 1867 vintage in particular. It was the restaurant's most famous vintage and one which they had particularly made sure to wall up in its entirety. Had that been a deadly mistake? Masson calmly told one of the most powerful men in the invading army that all of the vintage had, unfortunately, already been drunk. Göring insisted on a search and the troops searched the cellar for over two hours, checking every rack and box for some sign of the famous 1867 bottles. Finally, when they found nothing, they left – but they took all of the 80,000 bottles which remained in the open part of the cellar with them.

At the Hôtel de France in Champagne the owner had been less subtle and had hidden almost his entire cellar. On discovering that it was empty the troops who had had come to loot it went on a rampage, breaking all the furniture, smashing all the windows and hacking at the artwork on the walls. Despite their temper tantrum they never did discover the owner's hiding place. The champagne was stacked up inside the very walls of the historic building which they had reduced to a hollow wreck.

The owner of another château in Bordeaux had less success in keeping his wine hidden. He had very little time to hide his bottles after he heard that troops were on their way to be billeted at the château, where they were bound to raid his cellars. So he decided to sink his entire stock into his pond and for the first day everything went fine. Unfortunately, the labels from the bottles began to float to the surface overnight, the glue having been dissolved by the waters of their hiding place. In the morning the surface of the pond was carpeted with floating labels. The billeted officers rapidly realised where the missing wine was located.

As the occupation progressed, the looting of French wine became less violent and more systematic. A representative of the German government was appointed to each of the major wine-producing regions. It was their job to purchase wine for the German officials and the German forces to drink as well as wine to be exported and sold at a profit to support the costs of the war. While they were instructed to pay for the wine, they were also given wide-ranging powers to purchase compulsorily and at whatever prices were set by themselves and their superiors. The official name for the buyers was The Agents for Importing Wines from France, but the French just called them Weinführers.

In some areas the Weinführers were determined to work with the locals as fairly as they could. Heinz Bömers was appointed as the German representative in Bordeaux because he had worked as a wine importer for years and knew the region well. In fact, he had owned a château there before the French government confiscated all German property in France prior to the First World War. It might have been expected that he would hate the French for the loss of his château, but in fact it was the Nazis he hated. His brother-in-law, a Lutheran pastor, had been arrested and threatened with the death penalty simply for saying a prayer for the Jews at the end of his services. But he accepted the role as he wished to do what he could to protect his friends and long-time business partners from exploitation, knowing that if he did not accept the role then someone less sympathetic would be sent to do the job instead.

Throughout the occupation Bömers used his authority to ensure that no troops were able to loot the stocks of wine

and that any wine which was taken was paid for, even if it was at a lower price than would have been paid in peace-time. When buying wine for the main body of the armed forces, not the officers who might notice the difference and would be dangerous men to upset, he also ensured that the Bordelais were able to offload the poor-quality wine which had been produced in the bad harvests of the 1930s. It was such bad wine that they would otherwise have struggled to sell it at all.

When it was suggested to him that orders placed by German officials for specific grands crus should be ful-filled with cheaper wines; however, he refused to be a part of the plot. The danger of being caught was too great and the punishment would be too severe for himself and for the winemakers. He made only one exception to that rule because Bömers had an especial hatred for Göring. He regarded Göring as 'a pretentious thug whose evil is matched only by his greed', and so when Göring placed an order for several cases of Château Mouton Rotheschild he had a plan. The Weinführer had cases of *vin ordinaire* shipped to that château and told the workers there to paste Mouton labels on the bottles. As he had predicted, Göring's greed was not matched by his palate and he never even noticed the difference between the label and the contents.

In Champagne they were less lucky in their assigned Weinführer, Otto Klaebisch. Otto had been an agent for several champagne brands in Germany before the war and he should have been on good terms with the locals, but he enjoyed his new-found authority over them too much. His first act on arriving in the region was to requisition one of the grands châteaux for his own use, turning the de Vogüe family out of their home. The next day he met with the unofficial head negotiator for the region, only to discover that it was Count Robert-Jean de Vogüe, the brother of the man he had just turned out of his home. Once they had decided that he was not on their side, the Champenoise used every trick they could think of to keep their best wines out of the hands of the Germans. The special bottles they were required to produce and stamp 'Reserved for the Wehrmacht', which totalled millions of bottes every week, were a particular target for offloading the very worst champagne.

Klaebisch would sometimes push back against the resistance of the producers. He banned one house from the list of suppliers for sending particularly bad wine, which would have left them with no income as they were also not allowed to sell to anyone else, but the champagne producers committee simply had wine from that house shipped out to and bottled at other houses and then gave them their share of the proceeds. Later, François Taittinger was arrested after he not only supplied poor champagne but also insulted Klaebisch when he was called in to explain himself. He was a huge figure in the community and his loss was a great blow, but the producers of champagne continued their small resistance and, as the war went on, they also became increasingly involved with the real Resistance.

The producers quickly discovered that significant military intelligence could be gleaned from the champagne orders placed by the Germans. They always liked to have champagne on hand before a major military offensive to reward the troops if they were victorious. The Champenoise were able to send advance warning to British intelligence of the invasion of Romania and of the beginning of the North African campaign. The caves of Champagne were also perfect for use as storehouses and refuges for members of the Resistance and the Count de Vogüe himself came to head the political wing of the Resistance for the whole of eastern France until his arrest by the Gestapo in 1943.

Wines ordered by the Germans were also subject to further theft and deception after they left the vineyards. In the later years of the occupation thefts from the trains were so common that Resistance groups sometimes discovered that others had already beaten them to the prize. One Resistance cell was thrilled to discover that a train headed to Berlin, which they had pillaged, was filled with Bordeaux wines of the best vintage years and from the greatest châteaux. Unfortunately, when they uncorked them they discovered that the fine wines had already been replaced with cheap rubbish.

Parisian restaurants found themselves a particularly unlikely helper for turning their new wines into old wines in the form of a carpet-cleaning company. Chevalier's were not just any carpet cleaners, they were the best carpet cleaners in Paris. Valuable and antique carpets were sent to them for cleaning from across the country, and often it was not just the carpets which were antique but also the dust, which had been in them for centuries. Rather than throw away this ancient dust, the firm packed it into bags and then shipped it out to the best Parisian restaurants. The *maître d'hôtel* would smear the dust onto brand new bottles of wine and then charge their German customers through the nose for them.

Despite the resistance from growers, over 320 million bottles of wine were shipped to Germany over the course of the war. It was a huge proportion of the country's production, but some good stocks still remained in France. As the tide of the war turned in 1944 it became apparent that there was a significant risk to the remaining bottles. The retreating army might destroy them rather than let the French have them back. In Bordeaux, Captain Ernst Kühnemann received orders from Berlin to blow up the city as he retreated. Kühnemann was a distant cousin of Louis Eschenauer, one of the city's most prominent wine merchants, and Louis had invited him to dinner the previous night to beg him not to destroy the city. The captain was torn about what to do: he did not want to destroy the city but he also feared disobeying orders. Luckily, the decision was taken out of his hands when one of his subordinates took it upon himself to save the city by blowing up the unit's entire stock of detonators.

Paris also survived the retreat intact when the general charged with the destruction of the city refused to obey orders and surrendered the city with only a couple of notable liquid casualties. The first of those came at the hands of the Resistance themselves who, desperate for bottles to make Molotov cocktails, discovered cases of Taittinger champagne in the cellar of the Préfecture de Police. It was with great regret that they uncorked many of those bottles and poured them down the drain in order to furnish themselves with the weapons they needed. Then later, when the occupying forces had left the city and the celebrations of the liberation of Paris began, German planes made a precision strike on the Halle aux Vins (Hall of Wines). The hall was the city's wine centre, where the biggest wholesalers stored their stocks, which the retreating troops had already tried and failed to commandeer. The Germans were still determined not to let the French have them back. Hundreds of thousands of bottles of the finest wines were reduced to nothing but glass slag.

As the German retreat continued across Champagne and Burgundy, one unit of French troops carefully directed their American allies to advance up the eastern side of the Rhône, where the lesser growths were, while they took the western side themselves. They wanted to ensure that the retreating army were given plenty of time to move out whenever they crossed one of the grands crus, ensuring that machine-gun fire would be necessary only in the vineyards of inferior quality. The Americans accused them of going slow on purpose and holding up the war effort, but the troops refused to be ashamed of their efforts to save their greatest vineyards.

The final, and possibly greatest, reclamation of French wine came when the French 5th Tactical Group entered Berchtesgaden, the favoured summer retreat of the German high command nestled high up in the Bavarian Alps. Everyone knew that Berchtesgaden was going to be a great prize because the very best of all of the art and treasure which the Nazis had systematically looted from France and from German Jews had been sent there. The French unit had already played a few sneaky tricks on the American unit they were attached to in order to slip away and be the first to enter Berchtesgaden. There was just one higher prize left for them to reach, the Eagle's Nest, the private mountaintop retreat which Hitler had built at the top of one of the peaks. It was accessible only through a lift shaft which had been tunnelled directly up through solid rock.

The lift inside the shaft had been sabotaged beyond repair, which meant that the troops had to go the long way round, scaling the mountainside to reach it. They were led by the young Bernard de Nonancourt, who had been selected by his commanding officer to lead the mission because he came from Champagne and so was presumed to know something about wine. The great vault door could not be unlocked so they blew it open with explosives. Inside they found great art and treasures but no wine. The cellar was deeper inside, behind a second huge steel door which also had to be blown, but carefully, using just enough explosives to grant entrance without destroying the bottles behind. When it stood just ajar Nonancourt slipped through the narrow gap with his flashlight to find over half a million of the finest wines France had ever produced.

Among them his attention was immediately drawn to a number of cases of 1928 Salon Champagne. He remembered how five years earlier, when he was working at Delamotte across the street, he had watched as German soldiers had hauled that very champagne from the cellars of Salon and driven it away. He couldn't believe that he was now going to be the one to take it home again, minus only one or two bottles to celebrate their grand liberation of the spirit of the nation.

THE FUTURE OF WINE

IT TOOK time for the European vineyards to fully recover after the Second World War. The wineries of the New World moved to challenge their dominance as they did, filling the gap left in the market as production failed to meet demand. Yet, despite finding good soil and growing good grapes, most wines from Australia, Africa and South America were still proving harsh and strong. No matter how good the grapes were, they couldn't produce the subtle flavours of Old World wines because of the uncontrolled fermentation which ran ahead too fast in the warmer climates.

It was the invention of efficient cooling systems for the wine vats in the early 1960s that allowed wineries in warmer climates to benefit from the beautiful ripeness of their grapes by controlling the speed of fermentation. It was California that took the lead and soon it was dotted with a mixture of commercial mass-production wineries, which covered thousands of acres, alongside hundreds of smaller operations which became known as boutique wineries. The quality of the liquid improved rapidly, but to get the bottles off the shelves and into glasses required a revolution in marketing.

French wines, which were popular in the United States, were seen as the true mark of quality and early American wines had all been given names which alluded to the traditional regions and styles of France. Every pinot noir was Burgundy and every sparkling wine was champagne but, even when they were excellent, the wines were still clearly different from their namesakes. They needed their own identity, but to ask the public to remember a whole new set of geographies unique to California would have been a great challenge.

Since so much of the focus of the new generation of Californian winemakers was on finding the right grapevine which would thrive in the right microclimate of their specific valley or hillside, it made sense that the new type of wine labelling which would eventually take off was labelling by varietal. French wines had traditionally been labelled only by region and, while growers and dealers in wine knew that those regional styles were largely determined by the predominant local varietals, these were not facts that the general public were thought to care about.

However, the varietal system of labelling gave growers a way to link wines back to their Old World origins, and to provide accompanying notes that a particular variety was originally predominant in this or that region, while also celebrating the wine as local, unique and distinct to their own region. Today even French wines are listed with their constituent grapes on wine lists, which would have been unthinkable in earlier times.

In Australia, the main problem for the local wine industry wasn't competing with imported wines, but a lack of interest in wine altogether from a nation mostly of beer drinkers. The hot climate always called for something cool and refreshing to go with a barbecue rather than a heavy red for a dinner party. It was a white wine which eventually became popular, made with German grape varieties but quite different from the dry wines those varieties had traditionally produced. Australian sunshine produced riper grapes than were ever seen in the cool German valleys. The modern combination of temperature-controlled vats with superfine filters which removed all residual yeast allowed new wine producers to make a sweeter, fruitier wine which was also still and stable. The result was a perfect competitor to a beer on a sunny day, to be quaffed in quantity. While Europeans largely looked down on this new development, especially when it was released in 3-litre boxes with taps, such a still, fruity wine might have delighted Dom Pérignon before his quest for the perfect wine style for champagne was perverted by English tastes.

New worlds also produced new varieties, which revealed their origins only after decades. Zinfandel seemed to emerge in California as a unique local variety, despite clearly being an import of some kind since it was still a

Vitis vinifera. At some point during the wine rush either an obscure variety had come in or a cross had been produced and forgotten before being found again. The mystery origin of the vine did not prevent it from becoming wildly popular because of the easy-drinking white and rosé it produces. In fact, by the 1970s it may even have been the unique Californian nature of the variety which helped increase its popularity.

It took some genetic detective work to track down the origin of Zinfandel. It was found to be extremely similar to the Italian Primitivo, traditionally used in southern Italy to make red wine rather than white, but not quite similar enough to be the same grape. Instead the results hinted at a common ancestor to both varieties, which was eventually tracked down to an obscure Croatian grape variety, Crljenak Kaštelanski, also traditionally used to make red wine. Given the difficulty Americans would have in pronouncing the name, it's not surprising that Zinfandel became the more popular term for the grape. The use of the variety to produce sweet whites and rosé wines also remains uniquely Californian.

In contrast, the transformation of French Syrah into Australian Shiraz may have been a more intentional marketing ploy by the original importer of the vine, who was none other than the Scotsman James Busby. He imported the vine from the Hermitage vineyard in southern France, where he had been told local stories about the supposed

Iranian origin of the vine. Shiraz is a city in southern Iran and whether the name was changed because he believed that was the true origin of the vine or just to inject an exotic flavour into the marketing of the variety we don't know.

If it was the former, he was wrong. DNA testing has found no connection between Syrah and the vines growing around the modern city of Shiraz. Instead the vine was proven without doubt to be a native of southern France. However, the popularity the wine has enjoyed worldwide under the Australian name of Shiraz has been much wider than that of the French Syrah. The variety is most often used as a minority grape for blending and, although the blends which include it are famous names, such as Châteauneuf-du-Pape, the contribution of Syrah is generally forgotten against the primary Grenache grape. Australia uniquely popularised it as a grape variety for drinking on its own.

South Africa also has a unique variety of its own and, unlike Zinfandel and Shiraz, it actually originated in the country as a result of local experiments in cross-breeding. Pinotage is a cross-breed of Pinot Noir and Cinsault and, while it is very popular in South Africa, it is not well known elsewhere. While Australia and California were busy establishing their new varietals at a time of changing worldwide tastes in wine, South African products were largely still subject to boycott. By the time Apartheid ended in the 1990s, world tastes had become more static again and harder to change. So Shiraz and Chardonnay were planted for the already established world markets and this unique local wine was grown only in small quantities for local appreciation.

The other largest exporter of wine from the New World has no single unique variety of vine to its name, but all of its wines are in a way unique. Surrounded on all sides by natural barriers – oceans, deserts and high mountain ranges – Chile has managed to remain entirely free of phylloxera. While small patches of old vines in other parts of the world have remained unaffected, often commanding high prices for their unique wines, Chile is the only country in the world which produces all its wines on original, ungrafted *Vitis vinifera* vines. While it has long been established that grafting does not affect taste there remains something intangibly special about knowing that the wine in your glass comes from whole vines.

While Australia, South Africa, Chile and the United States of America remain the world's largest exporters of New World wine there is barely a corner of the world where vines will grow that wine is not produced, much of it fine and unique. Snowy Canada is able to produce icewines every year, whereas in Germany and Austria, where they are traditionally produced, only the very coldest winters produce icewines. At the other extreme, the Atlantic island of Fogo had a wine industry which suffered a major setback in 2014 when the volcano which formed the island erupted, destroying all of the vines which had been planted right inside the crater.

Back in the Old World a new guard of winemakers have reacted against what they see as the increasing industrialisation of winemaking, in particular the cooling systems and filters which made wine production possible worldwide and which eventually fed back into European wine production. The natural wine movement seeks to make wine from vine to glass with the minimum of intervention. That the definitions and standards of what exactly this means vary wildly from producer to producer is part of the industry's charm. Whether the makers are eschewing added sugar and yeast in sparkling wine to make the slightly cloudy Pétilliant Natural wines, affectionately known as Pét-Nat, or leaving the juice of green grapes sitting on the skins to produce characterful orange wines, you can be sure that unique and interesting things will come out of the movement.

As for the future of wine, the increasing popularity of wine in China, the most populous country in the world, must surely have an impact which cannot yet be predicted. Traditionally, grape wine has largely been ignored in China except as an occasional prestige purchase, imported at great expense, but over the last 20 years demand has increased significantly. By 2013 the country had become the world's largest consumer of red wine. The local industry has been working rapidly to catch up with consumption over the same period, more than doubling the area under vine and beating out France with the second largest area of vines in the world by 2014.

As in any demand-driven boom, quality lagged initially, but two wines were awarded China's first Decanter World Wine Awards gold medals in 2017. The following year eight golds were awarded to Chinese wines from a range of regions and in a range of styles. Where the continued steady increase in demand, production and quality will take China, and the world with it, is impossible to predict.

But the last word, sadly, must go to climate change. Despite the success that we have had in bringing the vine to a wide variety of situations and climates, its spread has been achieved by careful selection of growing areas within a country and by bringing in suitable varieties to match the growing conditions. The vine itself is a delicate and sensitive plant and established vineyards react strongly to variations in temperature. This sensitivity to small changes in temperature results in the variations in vintages which have always fascinated enthusiasts but also puts wine as we know it in great danger from climate change.

Droughts are already impacting harvests in South Africa and southern California. Only a small further increase in global temperatures could see venerable Bordeaux lose its viability as a growing region, along with the port-growing Douro and all but the highest slopes of Italian vineyards. Many of these regions could be retained with a change in varietals, but that would change the character of the wine and, because of naming rules that are intended to protect the unique character of the industry, vineyards could lose the right to use their own regional names. However, on the other side of that thin band around the world of areas with ideal growing temperatures other areas are warming up which have previously been too cold for winemaking.

The emergence of a strong British wine industry has often been attributed to consumer choice and the increased value placed on local products. But the simple fact is that, while it was not suitable before, Britain has become a viable place to grow wine as it has warmed. The French champagne house Taittinger has already planted a vineyard in Kent and others have made significant purchases of land against the day when they are needed. When a champagne house has lasted almost 300 years it gets used to planning for the long term, even if those plans may eventually involve moving out of France altogether.

Almost every vine in the world was replanted once, with new roots, over a hundred years ago. If every vine must be replanted again, just a little further north, then humanity will find a way to do it. We have grown wine for as long as we have grown anything at all and for as long as we grow anything at all we will continue to grow wine.

FURTHER READING

Christy Campbell, *Phylloxera: How Wine was Saved for the World* (New York: Harper Perennial, 2010).

Ian Gately, *Drink: A Cultural History of Alcohol* (London: Gotham Books, 2008).

Hugh Johnson, *Vintage: The Story of Wine* (New York: Simon & Schuster, 1989).

Don & Petie Kladstrup, *Wine and War: The French, the Nazis, and the Battle for France's Greatest Treasure* (London: Hodder and Stoughton, 2001).

Alex Liddell, *Madeira: The Mid-Atlantic Wine* (London: C. Hurst & Co., 2014).

Patrick E. McGovern, *Ancient Wine: The Search for the Origins of Viniculture* (Woodstock: Princeton University Press, 2003).

LIST OF ILLUSTRATIONS